THE SELF UNSTABLE

The Self Unstable
by Elisa Gabbert

Black Ocean
Boston · New York · Chicago

Black Ocean
P.O. Box 52030
Boston, MA 02205
blackocean.org

ISBN 978-0-9844752-9-2

Cataloging in Publication data
available at the Library of Congress

FIRST EDITION

TABLE OF CONTENTS

ACKNOWLEDGMENTS

Thanks to the editors of the journals where portions of this manuscript previously appeared, sometimes in earlier versions: *Another Chicago Magazine, Apt, The Awl, Barrelhouse, Boog City, Boston Review, Catch Up, Color Treasury, Dark Sky, Denver Quarterly, Esque, Everyday Genius, The Offending Adam, RealPoetik, The Rumpus, Sentence, Sink Review, So & So Magazine,* and *The Volta.*

I send love and gratitude to friends and family who read this book in manuscript form and have otherwise supported me, most especially John Cotter, my parents, Liz Hildreth, Kathy Rooney, Chad Reynolds, Dan Boehl, Jen Olsen, Janaka Stucky, and Carrie Olivia Adams.

"I often have to remind myself that my name is not Elise"
— Fani Papageorgiou, "Für Elise"

"What was the self?"
— Wallace Shawn, *The Designated Mourner*

What was the self?

You wanted a life of causes, but it was all effects: you could never get *before.*

Finding meaning in the meaningless was no kind of meaning, but you were satisfied with meaning*ness.*

Luck is a skill, as is beauty, intelligence—all things you're born with. It can almost ruin you, the belief that you can choose.

I watch a baby in a restaurant playing with a plastic Slinky.

The only way past is through.

THE SELF IS UNSTABLE:

HUMANS & OTHER ANIMALS

Memory comes first, then identity shortly after, at age 7 or 8. I wanted to be pretty, and now I am. Did wishing make it so? That I am *I* is less shocking than its opposite, that you are *you*. One day in my 20s, sitting in a cold car, I realized the self is universal, there is only one *I*—again, the thought arrives, but no longer seems profound.

Kittens are cuter than babies, an indication that they're using us for propagation at an advanced level. Our enemies are better for our art than our friends. Forgive me if I fabricate tension. Forgive me if I'm only capable of incomplete and indirect apologies. This is a negotiation, but I've got the weaponry.

Don't just be yourself—build your personal brand. The self is unstable. It might not be found by the search engines. It might be rejected. The self regenerates every five or six days. A consistent brand, a coherent self. Consider the interface, testing for usability. Even crows have a sense of self, and the accompanying self-esteem, self-loathing. The crow is self-reflexive, self-defeating. How dejected is the crow.

Animals can think about thinking, a grand failure of evolution. The best experiences involve no thinking at all, much less self-reference, much less an endless/strange loop. Whatever you do, don't start thinking about thinking.

Crows can tell one human from another, but we are unable to distinguish among various crows. This is mischaracterized as a paradox. Humans may be racist, but crows can't read, and robots can't really dance. All species evolve toward overspecialization. If you find anything other than food or sex interesting, it's signaling.

Satori is the first step toward "seeing your self-nature." This probably involves avoiding mirrors. I met a woman who is writing a novel about goodness. I told myself, "Be thankful for your enemies; they make you more yourself." I know nothing about Buddhism. I believe I am good. To have enemies is a coming of age. Do I want to be loved or misunderstood?

Whether humans or dolphins are more intelligent is academic. The common gray squirrel and zebra mussels are winning. Technology has advanced to the point that our generation could theoretically live indefinitely. This too is academic—asteroids, the switching of the poles, zebra mussels in the pipes. The technology will be destroyed.

Human life is structured around overcoming problems, primarily hunger. In America, the abundance of food is itself the problem. Other nations report more faith in marriage, but do it far less. They too die, but of simpler things. Great costs, like great pain, are eventually forgotten. I don't want kids, but there's nothing else to do.

"The paralysis of choice" is a theory based on one crappy study that has never been reproduced. Still, it's probably true. I'd rather make the wrong choice than make the right one and not know it. Regret is a kind of certainty. I used to say I never had regrets. I didn't realize I just didn't have any yet.

I saw a figure from a distance and thought it was me. I drank from the opposite side of a glass. If you can't describe how you feel to yourself, you can't be sure what you're feeling—or that you feel at all. Consciousness as unreliable narrator. The self is a play that you watch from the audience—you affect it, but you can't control it.

TRANSCENDING THE BODY:

MEMORIES, DREAMS, FEARS, & FANTASIES

Topologically, you're genus 1, same as a donut. Transcending the body sounds a little '80s to me, not to mention flaky and paranormal. Even avatars have gender. They say hypnosis only works if you believe in it, but God works either way.

One of my earliest memories is of drinking a Coke and feeling like I'd finally arrived. No experience is complete until I narrate it to myself. The algorithm is simple; it's the input that's random. The best way to speed-read is to turn off your inner voice, your mind-brain duality.

If you suspect that your child is a genius, observe it carefully. Does it use abstract logic for problem solving and have a high curiosity level, an extraordinary memory, a vivid imagination, and an excellent sense of humor? These signs are often seen in geniuses. Always keep a control child nearby for comparison. I strongly suspect that I was the control child. My brother convinced me I wanted to be a boy. Or, because of my brother, I wanted to be a boy.

There's no respect without fear, but there is fear without respect. This is another way of saying that fear is everywhere, which is why it's so scary. No aspect of my life is free of marketing. We were wrong about the infinite possibilities. You have to choose between the pure idea and the blaze orange tree.

Most days we don't think about the war. We don't watch the news. What we don't know might hurt us, but we're protective of our pain. The life of the mind: Life is in our minds, and the news is outside. Life is tragic in real time, but the memories are farcical. What good does it do to feel the same things over and over, to rehearse the same pains? Where are the clouds of the mind? Where is the play within the play?

I read about a man with severe amnesia, unable to form new memories, his diary filled with entries like *I am awake for the first time. . . . This time, finally really awake*—the torment of perpetual now. I rarely transgress in a dream; I dream of the guilt that follows transgression. The weird double-bind of time: we don't act in accordance with consequence, but we'd do nothing if we wouldn't remember it. Our lives are lived in the past.

Among the new hells is paradoxical insomnia: By any reasonable standards you are sleeping, but you swear up and down you aren't getting a wink. Scientists have not determined if the fact that you don't remember your dreams is a symptom or the cause. Unable to participate in the self-sufficient therapy of dream journaling, you may impose a symbology on regular life. But in this world, a mirror/fox/getting shot doesn't mean anything.

As they get older, as the women's movement progresses, women report less happiness, or is it—a slight difference—more unhappiness? But, you can argue, there's more to life than being happy. Most people choose power over happiness. A man in a coma for 23 years was found to have been conscious the whole time. This is a variation on the fantasy of attending your own funeral. Most of the time, if you "don't want to know," you already do.

The last day of my 29th year, I woke up crying. "Despite myself." Youth is wasted, full stop. We trade awe for regret, beauty for truth. I'll remember forever how Brandon Shimoda threw his half-eaten ice cream cone in the trash: "This is *boring.*" Awe is nothing like shock. Time moves so fast I want it to move faster, make memories of you.

If luxury is obscene, all pleasures are obscene. The tyranny of matters of degree. Faux fur is cruel by way of reference to cruelty. In the moment, we value stability, but we prefer our painful memories. Happiness as intensity of experience. Don't you always "feel the way you feel"?

Voting is inherently good—it inures us to outcomes, to our statistical insignificance. "I vote every day by not having children." Our most frequently accessed memories are most likely to be wrong, not to mention streaked with light. Pride is the successful avoidance of shame.

I was bitten by a feral cat, who left her fang behind in my hand. My dream life has its own past, memories I only access when asleep. When something hurts in a dream, where do you feel the pain? Is there an analog in the real world? And likewise, for the beauty? If we can't change the past, regret is a waste of time, but not worry or longing. Still, I prefer regret. If time is a vector, we are passengers facing the rear of the train.

If information has replaced the story, what will replace information? We have arrived at the future, but its use is restricted to the military. UIs aspire to the uncanny valley. We don't *want* to get over Romanticism. The bankruptcy of collective memory. The etymology of "hi."

A CRUDE KIND OF PROGRESS:
ART & AESTHETICS

The word *sexy* is sexy. That's how culture works. All language is descriptive. If you're not "trying too hard" you're trying hard not to. Irony is seen as a filter on sincerity; in truth both irony and sincerity are filters. In its pure form the data is too powerful.

Celebrities in magazines say confidence is sexy. But then there's the myth of beauty without vanity. And then the fetishization of numbers, rationality. As if the mind, in its frailty, could transcend feeling. Bias is familiar, comfortable as a shadow. It's not necessary to be both beautiful and funny.

They slowed down Beethoven's *Ninth Symphony* so it stretched over 24 hours. The effect was of a continual climbing, with no resolution—just an ever-building terror, the slowest imaginable scream. In a state of heightened time, everything reduces to fear, a sublime fear. If life has any meaning, it comes at the end.

Which comes first, senseless violence or meaningful violence? I mean everything I say, because everything means. Don't speak to me of facts. I despise history as I despise current events. History is the news via consensus. And then they add mood music. Don't speak of the future. What hasn't happened can never happen. I want to live in the hypothetical, the unproved.

In our pursuit of the new, we must cultivate fear, where there was no need for it historically. We must devalue narrative, but this alone is not enough—we must lose our comprehension, as a man who goes colorblind loses his concepts of color, so eventually his dreams and even his memories are in grayscale. So too the construct of time. So too the one, coherent world. This isn't for art. It's for science.

Just another toxic event. We can't tell anymore what's natural and what's not, and we certainly can't care. But we develop a leftist aesthetic. But what if the truth isn't elegant? It's okay to confess, if you embed it in an incoherent system; make them think you're unreliable.

Swatch is now a luxury brand. Why this final loss of innocence? Everything was big in the '80s. A watch you could hang on your wall. Visible beads at the end of each eyelash. The "so what" school of criticism.

If it's cool to be a geek, we have lost our systems of meaning. This was always the goal. We seek methods of being terrified. We want it to be art, so we redefine art. Not every culture has kings, but the geek is universal.

For something to be great, it has to be inevitable, and therefore obvious. The fallacy is thinking that the obvious must be great. So goes the history of art. "Great" doesn't *mean* "capacious," but they often correlate. When assessing greatness, ask yourself how many pianos would fit inside.

According to quantum theory, there's a real possibility you could fall through the floor. In some worlds, you do. Statistically, most worlds are boring. Most worlds could be improved with radical editing. If you like karaoke, you'll love neo-benshi.

I used to wear a watch all the time—in my sleep, in the ocean. It's common to fetishize a bad habit. One can will oneself out of obsession, but will itself becomes obsessive. The sound of something spinning: a symbol of lapse. Like poetry and music, a lapse is about time. My memory doesn't speak—it screens like dailies in the background. When I stare at the white ceiling, what I see is my eyes.

A photograph, in contrast to a painting or a sculpture, is not a unique object, and therefore has no aura. It is difficult to view a photography exhibit in a museum and feel moved. It is difficult to feel moved in general. One finds oneself repeatedly accessing a single painful or poignant memory. To elicit full tears, one must revise history. One must willfully make of the thing a grotesquerie.

The best perfumes are completely abstract, but as in other artforms, amateurs are more interested in the photorealistic—they are, in fact, more interested in a representational object that is *just like* a rose (or a woman, or burnt toast) than those items themselves. Art, over time, makes a crude kind of progress, but toward what end? Art may improve our quality of life, but better art does not improve it more.

What I miss about childhood is awe—the filter of inexperience, without the further filter of inadequacy, shame. But shame, a friend told me, can be comforting. Adulthood is knowing that someone is watching, an increasing sensation of things being fixed. When I hear the song for the second time, what I like is its familiarity. It has not become more beautiful, nor have I gained access to its beauty.

In a movie culture there is no play within the play. Writers hope for good actors, but when the acting is good you don't notice the writing. The audience wants immersion, not realism; realism is no more immersive than reality and no more a genre. If truth is a sliding scale, one must test the extremes.

Poetry fails as art in that it is not a Veblen good. The more you charge for it, the more worthless it seems. Information wants to be free, but what about beauty? The sublime? Is art *about* anything? Whatever it is, it's not meaning.

It's not that beautiful people are better conversationalists; it's that nobody cares. One of the failures of the body is the ability to feel chronic pain. After two or three years, nothing's getting done. There is beauty in pain, when the subject is attractive to begin with. Likewise, pain in beauty. The mere presence of a mirror sways subjects toward more ethical decision-making.

A paragraph is a way of saying one thing over and over again. Books are an act of supreme redundancy. What's the difference between ambivalence and ambiguity? POV.

A visitor from the past would look around and mainly see an absence of hats. The primary purpose of fashion is to signal in-group conformism. If everyone walked around naked, it would be difficult to spot our natural allies. We grow attached to our enemies. We would rather they not apologize, which would obviate the reason to hate them.

Wanting people to go fuck themselves isn't the same as wanting to tell them to. The ignominy of living near a major landmark. If this were neo-benshi, I'd say something wise and make everyone laugh. I'd be on the outside. From in here, the music's incongruous, the food smells overwhelming.

In a moment of silence, thoughts may impose themselves on the silence. So it becomes necessary to avoid silence. Wear headphones on the train. The problem with the train is the beautiful girls who never notice me. I am only noticed by less beautiful girls. Would you rather be popular or infamous? Wrong choice.

FIRST-PERSON SHOOTER:

GAMES & LEISURE

Hobbies, for adults, are advanced forms of indirect consumerism. Kids have no money, so they play games like "House" and "School" evoking settings they will later resent. Awareness is the great human problem; most endings are ruined by knowing they are. It's not clear what role processing speed has in subjective experience. A game of chess may be played at long distance and extended over a lifetime. The total amount of fun is constant, but is it ever at any point perceptible?

In air hockey, accidentally scoring on yourself is the alt win condition. As we age it becomes more difficult to experience triumph without drinking or conquering nations. Stress ages us quickly, as does eating—really, a supreme irony. If we want to be happy, why are we so fond of sad endings?

Drunk driving makes life feel even more like a side-scrolling video game. In *Sleep Is Death*, one player controls the world the other player experiences. Talk about fucked up power dynamics. In classic gaming, you begin to suspect the machine is human. Here you suspect your friend is a machine.

People think of themselves as something behind their eyes. First-person shooter. It's fun to be the player, but boring to watch. Writing is narcissistic, but without narcissism we'd have nothing to read. We do most things only in order to say we've done them, an ethical alternative to lying. Your "desert island movie" is not the same as your favorite movie.

War is like Go. If you have to count your dead, no one really won. Have you played *The Game of Life* recently? It parallels adult life to an insulting degree. Do you say "ow" when you're alone? Our mothers die before us, so we evolved self-pity.

Hangovers worsen as we age, but our tolerance does not decrease accordingly. File this under design concerns, system-level. The definition of "binge drinking" is disturbingly lax. Most adults can't have fun without alcohol, but it's easy enough to redefine fun. If not the malleability of language, the source of the argument can often be traced back to dissatisfying sex.

In my sex tape the vocalist does an anagram-esque sequence like overheard speech in a foreign language. This takes place off-camera, but you can tell by the players' reactions the soundtrack's intrinsic. It's so cerebral it's not sexy, but for the paradox, the inherently sexy x. All games are dangerous. Schadenfreude complicates utilitarianism.

ENJOYMENT OF ADVERSITY:

LOVE & SEX

You can read a text just fine when the letters are out of order. This isn't "my best work." I admit I'm depressed for relief from depression; the effect doesn't last. *Be careful flâneuring around with someone who loves you.* Happiness should be all that matters, but it's not even high on the list. The hangover is one known form of regret that transcends culture.

Do you ever revert to a dialect of baby talk from a previous relationship? It's a coding error. It's a dick move. In uncomfortable situations one may rely on affected habits, on metajokes. Enjoyment of adversity is a sign of genius, but the mad genius is oblivious to adversity.

Girls want to be beautiful. Boys want to be powerful. In other words, everyone wants to be powerful. The appeal of Houdini and lingerie is the same: The more straps you wear, the nakeder you look. The only natural responses to vulnerability are love and violence.

We are both attracted to the older poet, but unsure if we'd prefer her as mother or lover. She calls us beautiful, in such a skilled and subtle way that we don't have to feign embarrassment or reveal how pleased we are, by blushing or saying thank you. She does not read from her book, which in any case isn't poetry, but fragments of a journal. The secrecy of diaries is pretense. One journals in the hope, the expectation, that someone will read it: the enemy, a future self, the still unborn. I like my mother, but you can only like your own mother so much. The more you love someone, the less you like them.

You lose naïveté before you gain wisdom. In the interim, you believe that everything is about sex. Your dreams are given to obvious motifs: the motif of your blows falling weak and ineffectual, glancing off the enemy. The motif of the foreign airport, being unable to pack, having nothing to wear. In dreams, even sex is symbolic of sex.

I love when men say the word *pretty*. Sex is a kind of overstatement, but men are most attractive when ambiguous. I like men to dislike me a little. Behind their aviators men might not be looking at you at all. They might be thinking about another woman entirely, or a man, or sex as a vague abstract. At any given time, most men are secretly thinking about sex. But some men, during sex, must think about music.

When the novelty of the new wears off, it feels chintzy. The way I feel about strangers is unconditional. They never seem strange. "Strange" has lost its original meaning; it now means "vague." I regret the mistakes I made in my 20s, though I am the same, and would make them again. In fact I wish I could make them again.

When you suspect someone is in love with you, you begin to treat them with contempt. Cruelty is justified, even an obligation. You engage in the feminism of rejecting your beauty. Nevertheless, you hope to remain attractive. In fact, you become more so. Men test the limits of your capacity for cruelty, follow you into bars.

My ex read about a woman who believed she was having orgasms, until she finally had a "real" one. He suggested my orgasms might not be real. What an odd way to undercut me, since he was the one providing them. Is it even possible to have an imaginary orgasm? If you believe you are happy, aren't you, for all intents and purposes, happy? Don't you always feel the way you feel?

He said it was "an elegant scar." My sex dreams are too realistic. We watch the sunset from a plane, and later, the city lights approaching in the dark, copper and green. Why are they all orange or green? *My enemy. My enemy.* If you tell me you love me, accidentally or automatically, I will always forgive you. How quickly the unexamined becomes the overexplained.

A shared taste in music is a sure sign of star-crossed romance. After late-stage denial, a misdirected searching moral inventory, then blame and other bad science. Correlation is not causation, but it's damning anyway. Death knells sound less final than you'd think.

Sexual tension must culminate or deteriorate; thus all passionate friendships end with resentment. Be careful what you do "with abandonment." In fantasies of sudden death, one's enemies are finally sorry; this only endears them to the fantasizer. Be careful what you wish for, in that it tells you what you want.

Men say infuriating things, and the fury has nowhere to go. The fury becomes ingrown. Your personality is a choice, so why are you half little-girl and unlike yourself? You don't change, exactly, but the wave amplifies. The world is your ulcer. Love turns blood-brown. Be careful what you say, in that it tells you what you think.

Be thankful for adversity. Boethius said, "For in all adversity of fortune the worst sort of misery is to have been happy." It's easier to repeat mistakes than re-create successes, so think of your past self as a different person—your past selves, different people. No great art comes from happiness or comfort, but discomfort isn't enough. I write from suffering, not lust.

Koans are used to provoke "the great doubt." Contentment isn't happiness. I told a student that desire comes from boredom. But I seek out desire, so why do I fear boredom? Maybe emotions *are* ideas. I believe in the end of history illusion, but I also believe in the end of history, the failure of all imagination. The future isn't anywhere, so we can never get there. We can only disappear.